COPYRIGHT

Cover design by Julia H. Sun

Although every precaution has been taken to verify the accuracy
of the information contained herein, the author and publisher
assume no responsibility for any errors or omissions. No liability is
assumed for damages that may result from the use of information
contained within.

This book contains information that is intended to help the
readers become better-informed consumers of health care. It is
not intended to be a substitute for the medical advice of a
licensed physician. The reader should consult with a doctor or
other medical professionals in any matters relating to his/her
health.

All trademarks in this book are the property of their respective owners.

First Edition

ACKNOWLEDGEMENTS

This *7-Day Incredible Meal Plan for Complete Health* is the result of many years of work. Without the help from my family, friends and many others, this book would not exist.

I'm blessed with having grown up in a loving, caring, and supportive family and with two wonderful sons, Tyler and Peter Lu. In the journey of writing this book, as well as healing all my illnesses and pursuing the other aspects of my life, my family has provided me with determination, patience, and perseverance, whether from my grandmother's heartfelt words of encouragement, my parents' nurturing love and support, seemingly endless conversations with my sisters and brothers, and my sons' invaluable assistance with ideas and the English language.

I am most appreciative of my Chinese ancestors' invaluable knowledge of health and well-being passed down through countless generations. It is the Chinese culture and philosophy of health and Traditional Chinese Medicine that saved my life. They made it possible for me to recover from illnesses and to share this knowledge with the world through my books, training programs, energy healings, public speeches, and the Total Life Energy Plan.

My sincere thanks go to Curt Hoffman. With his 30 years of engineering and business technical writing, along with his culinary background, Curt graciously finds time in his busy schedule to provide ideas and review the entire contents of this recipe book.

My special thanks also go to many friends, customers, and everyone else who helped with this book directly and indirectly, and who believe in me and the Total Life Energy Plan that can improve public health, change people's lives, and contribute to a better world.

Other Literatures Authored by Julia H. Sun

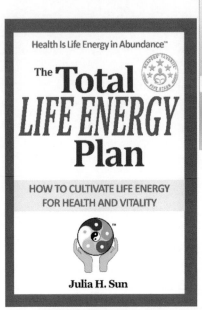
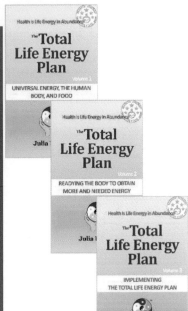

TABLE OF CONTENTS

The 7-Day Meal Plan

The 7-day Meal Plan

	Monday	Tuesday	Wednesday	Thursday	Friday	Saturday	Sunday
Breakfast	pancakes with honey corn mush with sesame seeds milk	bread with butter eggs black tea or black soy drink	crepes with chopped scallions sorghum porridge milk or black tea	ham, scallion, and cheddar omelet oatmeal with honey milk	bacon with egg sandwich oatmeal with brown sugar brown rice tea	five-color porridge bacon sandwich fermented vegetables	shaved steak omelet muffin milk
Morning Snack	almonds/ pine nuts/ boiled peanuts	walnuts	boiled peanuts with skin	roasted pumpkin/ sunflower seeds	roasted chestnuts or sweet potato	mixed nuts	mixed nuts
Lunch	stewed beef with daikon brown (and black) rice	noodles with chicken, potato, and mushrooms	beef with mustard greens bread or wheat bun	shredded steak sandwich with wheat bread	lamb stew with vegetables rice or wheat bun	burger	steamed meatballs
Dinner	pork rib rice soup with vegetables	wheat flake soup with beef	carrot and pumpkin paste	adzuki bean, rice, and millet porridge	rice soup with eggs and vegetables	black rice paste	rice soup with eggs and chicken broth

How to Use the Plan

1. In the 7-day Meal Plan, the meals of each weekday mainly nourish two of the Five Primary Organs, to which each organ and body part is directly related and connected in the body's energy system. Monday: Lungs/Liver; Tuesday: Kidneys/Heart; Wednesday: Liver/Spleen; Thursday: Heart/Lungs; Friday: Spleen/Kidneys. For each weekend day, eat for all Five Organs or your favorite foods. For detailed explanations of food properties, organs in the body's energy system, and foods and organ relationships, check out my book *The Total Life Energy Plan – How to Cultivate Life Energy for Health and Vitality*.

2. Please note that some ingredients, such as "beef", are used in more than one recipe. The properties and functions of these foods are mainly or only described in the first recipe. Refer to the Food Index for a list of foods with their energy properties.

3. Seafood often irritates an illness and aggravates the symptoms of an illness. If you are not ill, you can replace some meat with corresponding seafood. For example, have fried calamari (squid) with garlic for lunch for your Lungs on Mondays.

4. You can replace (muscle) meat with organ meat for your corresponding organs. For example, replace beef with beef liver for your Liver.

5. If you are hungry between lunch and dinner, have an afternoon snack that is suitable for your health

conditions. You can also substitute dinner with a snack or have no dinner.

6. You may cook ethnic meals with the same or similarly propertied foods. For example, replace "beef with mustard greens" with liverwurst.

7. Change the foods and meals to suit your body, your health, your living environment, and your culture. These are generic recipes yielding 2 or more servings each unless specified otherwise. Please change the ingredients and adjust the amounts or proportions of the ingredients as needed to better accommodate your own personal energy and health conditions following the Total Life Energy Plan as well as Traditional Chinese Medicine.

8. Be sure to select high quality all-natural organic food with no chemicals and artificial ingredients, and with as less processing as possible. High quality food provides more nourishment and needs much less body's resources on digestion and absorption as well as on processing wastes and toxins.

9. Always have good eating habits and never overeat. Hold two hands together to make a bowl. This bowl is about the size of your stomach. To be sure of eating the right amount, never have more than what that bowl might hold. For other eating habits and the detailed explanations, check out the Life Energy Diet online or in my book *Total Life Energy Plan – How to Cultivate Life Energy for Health and Vitality* (ISBN number 978-0999623237). The book is available on

Amazon, www.totallifeenergyplan.com, public libraries, and many other websites. (See Page IV for the cover of the book.)

DAY 1

Breakfast

    pancakes with honey

    corn mush with sesame seeds

    milk

Morning Snack:

    almonds/pine nuts/boiled peanuts

Lunch:

    stewed beef with daikon

    brown (and black) rice

Dinner:

    pork rib rice soup with vegetables

Pancakes with Honey

1 cup all-purpose flour
1 cup warm milk or kefir
2 medium eggs
¼ cup starter dough
1 tablespoon white sugar
½ teaspoon salt
2 tablespoons of unsalted butter, melted
3-4 teaspoon honey

1. In a large bowl, mix the flour, sugar, and salt together.
2. Mix the warm milk or kefir, melted butter, eggs, and starter dough. Then blend in the dry ingredients. Stir until no lumps remain.
3. Cover the bowl and keep it in a warm place to let the dough rise until doubled, 2-3 hours.
4. Heat a lightly oiled griddle or pan over medium heat. Drop 1/4-cup batter onto the griddle or into the pan and cook until bubbles form and the edges are dry, about 2 to 3 minutes. Flip and cook until browned on the other side, about 1 to 2 minutes. Repeat with remaining batter.
5. Serve warm with drizzled honey.

If using active dry yeast instead of starter dough, mix the yeast with warm milk and let stand for 5 minutes before mixing with other ingredients. Use an extra ¼ cup of flour.

pancakes

Functions:

Cow's milk is neutral to the human body's energy while goat and lamb milk is warmer than the human body. They all act on the Spleen, Lungs, and Heart, and provide blood, fluid, essence, and qi.

Egg yolk is neutral while egg white is cool. Egg white and yolk together act on the Spleen, Heart, Kidneys, and Lungs. Eggs nourish the body with essence and blood, calm the body and mind, including an overactive fetus, lubricate dryness, detoxify the body, and ease dry coughs, hoarse voice, dysentery, blood and yin deficiencies, and itches.

Wheat flour is cool and sweet. It provides qi and essence and acts on the Spleen and Heart. It nourishes the Heart, regulates qi, calms agitation and spirit, resolves dampness and swelling, controls excessive or abnormal sweating, relieves restlessness, and quenches thirst.

White sugar is neutral and sweet, acts on the Spleen and Lungs, and fortifies bodily fluid. It balances the Middle Warmer (the stomach and spleen area) and reduces overheating and inflammation. It relieves weakness in the middle part of the torso, pain and discomfort in the stomach area, dryness in the mouth and Lungs, and dry cough.

Salt is cold and salty and acts on the Kidneys, Stomach, Small and Large Intestines. It prevents dehydration, dissolves hard lumps, relieves congestion and constipation.

Butter is warm and sweet and provides qi. It assists in the treatment of a variety of ulcer and skin infections, such as fungal and mite infections.

Raw honey is neutral, while heated or cooked honey is warm. Honey is sweet and strengthens the Spleen, Stomach, Lungs, and Large Intestine. It nourishes yin, lubricates dryness, tonifies weakness, harmonizes the whole body, and detoxifies bodily waste.

These pancakes are a well-balanced dish that acts on all Five Organs and provides all Five Basic Substances.

Corn Mush with Sesame Seeds

½ cup stone-ground cornmeal
3 cups water and 1 cup milk
1 tablespoon sesame seeds, toasted and ground

1. Mix the cornmeal and water in a pot. Bring to a boil over high heat, stirring constantly.
2. Reduce to medium heat and cook until mushy, about 10 minutes.
3. Stir in the ground sesame seeds.
4. Add milk.
5. Serve warm with brown sugar, ground ginger, or cinnamon as needed.

corn mush with sesame seeds

Functions:

Corn is neutral and sweet and acts on the Lungs and Spleen. It tonifies qi, stimulates appetite, strengthens the stomach and spleen, and has a drying effect. It is for urinary difficulties, edema, diabetes, high blood pressure, diarrhea, indigestion, hyperlipidemia, and constipation.

Sesame seeds are close to neutral and sweet. They strengthen the Liver and Kidneys, nourish blood and essence, lubricate the intestines, and moisten dryness. They are for blurred vision, dizziness, tinnitus, premature graying hair, recovery from long-term illness, breast milk production, headaches, and numbness. They are also for constipation or dry stools due to a lack of yin or blood.

Corn mush with sesame seeds is a traditional Chinese breakfast. With milk, it fortifies the nourishment on the Lungs, Liver, and Kidneys.

Boiled Peanuts with Skin

1 cup peanuts with skin
2-3 petals of star anise
1 teaspoon salt

1. Place peanuts, star anise, and salt in a pot. Add enough water to cover and bring to a boil.
2. Simmer for about 30 minutes until peanuts are fully cooked and the inside is soft.

boiled peanuts with skin

Functions:

Star anise is warm, sweet, and spicy. It acts on the Liver, Kidneys, Spleen, and Stomach. It expels cold, aids in qi circulation and easing the pain and discomfort caused by cold and dampness.

Peanuts are neutral and sweet. They improve appetite, strengthen the Spleen, lubricate the Lungs, help with dry cough and dry stools, and aid in lactation. Peanut skin is neutral, sweet, bitter, and sour (astringent). It acts on the Liver, as well as the Spleen and Lungs. Peanut skin has many functions, such as regulating blood, helping to stop bleeding, dissolving stagnant blood, reducing swelling, and should not be discarded.

star anise

Stewed Beef with Daikon

1 lb stew beef
1/3 lb daikon
¼ cup all-purpose flour
1 to 2 teaspoons cooking or red wine
2 tablespoon chopped scallions
1 to 2 slices ginger
1 tablespoon butter or vegetable oil
1 teaspoon salt

1. Toss the meat in the flour until coated.
2. Heat the butter or oil in a large nonstick skillet or Dutch oven over medium-high heat. Shake off excess flour from the beef and add the beef to the pot. Brown the beef on all sides, about 4 -5 minutes. Remove the browned beef to a large bowl.
3. Add water, ginger, scallions, and cooking wine to the skillet or Dutch oven. Bring to a boil. Then add the browned beef. (Make sure there is enough water to cover the beef.) Simmer until beef is tender, about an hour.
4. Cut daikon into proximately 1 1/2-inch cubes.
5. Add salt and daikon cubes and simmer until daikon is cooked, about 20 minutes.

daikon

Functions:

Beef is neutral (or a little warm) and sweet. It provides qi and blood, strengthens the Spleen and Stomach, dispels dampness, and strengthens bones and tendons. It helps with edema, abdominal distention and fullness, weak back and knees, and deficient Stomach and Spleen.

Daikon is cool, pungent, and sweet. It acts on the Spleen and Lungs, removes stagnant food, moistens lungs, resolves mucus, quenches thirst, and relieves alcohol intoxication. It is for bronchitis, sore throat, dry cough, coughing with blood, painful urination, excess of mucus, alcohol intoxication, and food retention.

Scallions are warm and spicy. They act on the Lungs, Stomach, Liver, and eyes. They have many functions, including increasing yang, inducing sweating, expelling cold, brightening the eyes, helping energy distribution and circulation in the body including muscles, joints, and the middle warmer, helping the Liver cleanse poisons in the body especially from medications, seafood, and meat, regulating waste elimination through urination and bowel movements, and easing both constipation and diarrhea.

Fresh ginger is warm and spicy, *dry ginger* is hot and spicy, and *ginger skin* is cool and spicy. Ginger acts on the Spleen, Stomach, Lungs, and Heart, promotes circulation and sweating, expels cold, wind, and dampness, and releases toxins and seafood poisoning. It is for common colds, coughing with clear or white mucus, vomiting, diarrhea, and arthritis. Ginger skin acts on the Spleen and Lungs, regulates bodily fluids, induces urination, and relieves edema and a bloated stomach.

Wine is warm, spicy, bitter, and sweet, and acts on the Heart, Liver, Stomach, and Lungs. It improves circulation and expels cold and wind. It also can be poisonous if consumed in excess.

This dish is a popular winter dish in China for fortifying qi, nourishing the Lungs, warming the body in the cold, and cleansing stagnant air and food in the digestive tract.

stewed beef with daikon and the rice for lunch

Pork Rib Rice Soup with Vegetables

1 lb pork ribs in 1-inch strips
½ cup uncooked white rice
1 carrot
½ lb sugar pumpkin, optional
½ ear of corn, optional
¼ cup white scallions, sliced into 1-inch-long pieces
1 tablespoon green scallions, chopped into small pieces
2 to 3 thinly sliced pieces of ginger
2 to 3 Shiitake mushrooms
4 cups water

1. Remove the pumpkin skin. Cut the pumpkin and carrot into about 1 ½ inch chunks; slice the ear of corn into 1-inch slices; and thinly slice the ginger.
2. Rinse the pork ribs and blanch in boiling water for 3 to 5 minutes till the foam is floating. Remove the foam and rinse the pork ribs again.
3. Add the water to a pot and bring it to a boil.
4. Add the pork ribs, white scallion pieces, ginger slices, and mushrooms. Bring to a boil again. Then simmer on low for 1 hour.
5. Add carrot, pumpkin, corn, and rice. Simmer until both the rice and carrots are tender, about 30 minutes.
6. Turn off the heat, add salt to taste, and sprinkle with green scallions when it is ready to serve.

pork rib rice soup with vegetables

Functions:

Pork is neutral, sweet, and salty. It acts on the Spleen, Stomach, and Kidneys. It is for dry cough, constipation, too thin a body caused by illness and weakness, and a bodily fluid deficiency from excess heat in the body.

Pumpkin is warm and sweet. It acts on the Spleen, Stomach, Lungs, and Heart. It moistens and nourishes organs, tonifies qi, strengthens the Middle Warmer. It reduces swelling and helps the body remove poisons, especially from bee bites and medications.

Rice is neutral and sweet. It provides qi, moistens yin, clears heat, dries up loose stools, reduces swelling. It helps with weakness in the Stomach and Spleen, febrile diseases, swelling, nausea, and diarrhea.

Brown rice is also neutral and sweet. It strengthens the Spleen, Stomach, and Lungs, relieves irritability, eases loose stools. It helps with indigestion, diarrhea, vomiting, nausea, and being irritated by heat. Brown rice is packed with more nutrition and is much harder on the digestive system than white rice. If using brown rice, soak the rice in water overnight and add it early to the pot, together with the blanched pork ribs.

Shiitake mushrooms are neutral and sweet and act on the Stomach and Liver. They nourish the Stomach qi, increase appetite, and support a body that is weak and lacking in strength. They cleanse toxins and prevent tumors.

Carrots are sweet. Raw carrots are cool, but when cooked are neutral. Carrots act on the Spleen, Lungs, and Liver. They clear heat, detoxify bodily waste, strengthen the Spleen, Liver, the eyes, and a weak body, and relieve cough and measles.

Onions are warm, sweet, and spicy. They act on the Stomach, help the body circulate qi, cleanse waste gas, kill germs, and expel dampness.

This dish nourishes yin, fortifies yang, replenishes essence and blood. It is suitable for qi, blood, and yin deficiencies. But people with damp and heat symptoms such as being overweight, coughs with discharge, and high blood lipids should be careful and should not have too much.

Sayings on Medicine and Food:

> *Let food be thy medicine and medicine be thy food.*

Hippocrates, ancient Greek physician, (460-377 BC)

> *When diet is wrong, medicine is of no use. When diet is correct, medicine is of no need.*

Ayurvedic saying

> *If it is medicine, it contains toxic components.*

Chinese saying

DAY 2

Breakfast:

    bread with butter

    hard-boiled or scrambled eggs

    black tea or black soy drink

Morning Snack:

    walnuts

Lunch:

    noodles with chicken, potato, and mushrooms

Dinner:

    wheat flake soup with beef

Black Soy Drink

1/2 cup dried organic black (or yellow) soybeans
3 cups water for soaking
5 to 6 cups water for blending
1 teaspoon salt

1. Soak soybeans in 3 cups of water overnight until the beans expand and most of the water has been absorbed.
2. Discard water, remove remaining hard (un-expanded) soybeans and loose skins, and rinse.
3. Add the soaked soybeans and enough water (2 or more cups) to a blender or food processor. The amount of water added depends on the type and size of your blender or food processor. Add the rest of water during or after blending. Blend until smooth.
4. Strain the blended mixture through cheesecloth or a strainer, squeezing out as much liquid as possible into a pot that is tall enough to prevent overflow when boiling.
5. Heat the pot uncovered over medium-high heat. Keep an eye on the liquid because it will suddenly start bubbling and may boil over. Heat until the liquid starts to boil and becomes very foamy.
6. Reduce the heat to low and keep stirring and skimming foam so that it does not boil over.
7. Once the liquid stops boiling, increase to medium-high heat again and bring to boil.
8. Repeat Steps 6 and 7 a couple of times until the liquid suddenly stops bubbling and boiling on high heat. The boiling is not real boiling but is the escape of harmful gases, containing trypsin inhibitor and saponins, from the

liquid at a temperature of about 176F (80C). This is lower than the regular boiling temperature of 212F (100 C). It is called false boiling.

9. Keep on high heat until the liquid starts to boil (real boiling now) and boil for a minute or two.
10. Add a little salt to taste. Serve warm.

Functions:

Black soybeans are neutral, sweet, and salty. They act on the Spleen and Kidneys. They tonify the Kidneys, nourish yin, strengthen and nourish blood, and remedy Kidney deficiencies. They relieve lower back pain, knee pain, infertility, seminal emissions, blurry vision, ear problems, and urinary problems. Make sure the beans are ground and thoroughly cooked to avoid any harmful or unpleasant effects.

black soy drink   yellow soy drink

Noodles with Chicken, Potato, and Mushrooms

1 lb fresh noodles (made from about 2 cups of flour)
1 lb chicken, boneless, skinless (breast, thighs, or legs),
   cut into thin strips
1-2 potatoes, cut into strips
3-4 fresh shiitake mushrooms, thinly sliced
1-2 tablespoons butter, lard, or peanut oil
1 tablespoon finely shredded or chopped ginger
1 tablespoon cooking wine
2 teaspoon thickener (wheat flour or cornstarch)
1 tablespoon soy sauce
2-3 tablespoons of scallions, white and green parts
   separated and chopped.
salt to taste

1. Put chicken in a bowl and add ginger, cooking wine, thickener, soy sauce, and salt. Mix gently to combine. Set aside.
2. Cook noodles in boiling water over a high heat until just done, 3 to 5 minutes, stirring to prevent sticking. Drain water out of the noodles. You may rinse the noodles with cool water until the noodles cool to prevent the noodles from continuing to cook and sticking together. Shake well to remove water.
3. Heat the fat or oil in a frying pan. Add chopped white scallions and stir 10 seconds. Add chicken and stir-fry for 3 to 5 minutes. Remove chicken to a bowl. Add the potatoes, mushrooms, and seasonal vegetables to the pan and cook for another 2-3 minutes until done.

4. Add chicken, noodles, and chopped green scallions. Stir constantly for a minute or until all ingredients are well-mixed and heated through.

noodle with chicken, potato, and mushrooms

Functions:

Chicken is warm and sweet, acts on the Stomach and Spleen, and provides essence, qi, and fluid. It nourishes blood and aids in Kidney deficiencies. It is good for postpartum weakness, lack of energy and strength, and the weakness after illness.

Potatoes are neutral and sweet. They strengthen the Spleen, harmonize the Stomach, invigorate qi, detoxify poisons, and relieve infections and edema.

Peanut oil is neutral and sweet. It moisturizes the body heat, lubricates the digestive tract, and eases fullness and bloating caused by indigestion.

Soy sauce is a liquid condiment made by fermenting soybeans, wheat, and/or bran. It is cold and salty. It is used to enrich food color, flavor and taste, stimulate digestive functions, and bring food to the Kidneys.

Wheat and *eggs* nourish the Heart.

This dish nourishes the Kidneys and Heart, as well as the Spleen and Lungs which generate and supply energy to the whole body, including the Kidneys and Heart.

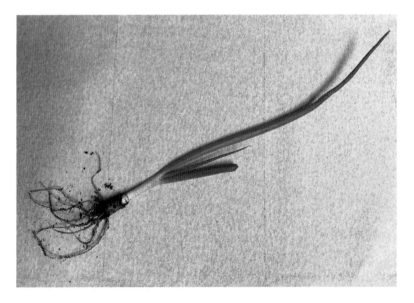

scallion

Noodles

2 cup all-purpose flour
½ cup water
1-2 eggs
¼-½ teaspoon salt (optional)

1. Combine the flour, water, eggs, and salt in a large bowl to make a dough. Knead by hand until the dough becomes soft and sticks together firmly, about 5 minutes.
2. On a lightly floured board, roll the dough into a paper-thin rectangle. Dust both sides of the dough with flour to prevent sticking while rolling.
3. Roll dough, jelly-roll style. Cut the dough into 1/4-inch (or thinner) slices with a knife. Unroll noodles. Dust with more flour to keep noodles from sticking together.
4. To cook, bring water to a rapid boil. (Optional: add salt and 1 tablespoon oil into water). Drop noodles into boiling water and cook until they float or are tender but not too tender, about 3-5 minutes.

rolled dough   cut and unrolled

Wheat Flake Soup with Beef

1 cup all-purpose flour
3/8 cup water
¼ teaspoon salt
1 teaspoon fat or vegetable oil
¼ lb ground beef
5 cups broth, made from beef bone marrow
2 tablespoons chopped scallions
*2 leaves from a seasonal vegetable, such as cabbage and
    Napa cabbage, torn into 1-inch pieces*
1 tablespoon soy sauce
1 teaspoon sesame oil

1. Combine the flour, water, salt, and oil in a large bowl to make dough. Knead by hand for about 5 minutes until the dough becomes soft and sticks together firmly.
2. Add ground beef and broth to a pot and bring it to a boil. Add the seasonal vegetable.
3. Make the flakes: Put the dough in your left hand and pull and stretch it with your right hand. Get it as thin as possible. Then tear a bite-sized piece off with your right hand. Drop the piece into the boiling soup. Repeat this with the remaining dough.
4. Cook until noodles float to the surface, about 2 minutes.
5. Add soy sauce, scallions, and sesame oil. Serve.

*Tip: If you make more than a double recipe, tearing the dough may take too long. You may roll the dough into a flat, thin disc and then tear or cut it into pieces.

wheat flake soup with beef

Functions:

Beef bone marrow is warm and sweet, acts on the Kidneys, Heart, and Spleen. It provides essence, nourishes the Kidneys, builds bones, and helps with bleeding.

Sesame oil is sweet and cool. It acts on the Large Intestine and helps with bowel movement, cleansing body toxins, including the toxins generated by excess body heat, food, bugs, and germs.

This dish nourishes the Kidneys, Heart, and Spleen.

Sayings on the Importance of Health:

> *The first wealth is health.*

Ralph Waldo Emerson, American philosopher, 1803 – 1882.

> *Take care of your body. It's the only place you have to live.*

Jim Rohn, author and motivational speaker, 1930-2009

DAY 3

Breakfast:

crepes with chopped scallions

sorghum porridge

milk or black tea

Morning Snack:

boiled peanuts with skin (*See Day 1, Page 17*)

Lunch:

beef with mustard greens

bread or steamed wheat bun

Dinner:

carrot and pumpkin paste

Crepes with Chopped Scallion

1 cup all-purpose flour and ¼ starter dough, or
1 ¼ cups all-purpose flour and 1 teaspoon active dry
*   yeast*
2 eggs
¼ cup milk or kefir
¼ cup chopped green scallions
1 teaspoon salt
½ cup warm water
2-3 tablespoons butter or lard, melted

1. Combine flour, eggs, yeast or starter dough, salt, chopped scallions, and water in a bowl and mix well to form a batter. If using starter dough, you may need less flour or more water to make a batter.
2. Heat 1 teaspoon fat in a skillet, griddle, or frying pan over medium heat until warm. Spread the fat over the bottom of the pan.
3. Pour or ladle batter into pan, using about 1/4 cup for each crepe, and use a spatula to spread the batter into a thin, round crepe.
4. Cook each side until it is light brown, about 1 minute.
5. Repeat 2 – 4 for the rest of the batter. Serve warm.

Functions:

Green scallions act on the Liver. Both *egg white and yolk* act on the Spleen.

Lard is sweet and neutral and acts on the Large Intestine and Lungs. It energizes the body and helps with dry cough, constipation, and dry itchy skin.

This dish nourishes the Liver and Spleen, as well as the other organs, and helps the Liver and Large Intestine to cleanse wastes.

crepes with chopped scallion

Sorghum Porridge

1 cup sorghum flour
4 ½ cups water
2 teaspoons sugar
a little milk, if desired

1. Mix the sorghum flour with water in a pot. Bring it to a boil, stirring constantly until it starts to bubble.
2. Depending on how finely the sorghum is ground, cook for 5-15 minutes until smooth and thick, stirring occasionally.
3. Add sugar and serve warm.
4. Add a little milk for a slightly creamier taste.

If using whole sorghum instead of sorghum flour, soak sorghum overnight and simmer for about an hour until the sorghum turns soft and is mixed together with liquid.

Functions:

Sorghum is warm, sweet, and sour (astringent). It nourishes the Liver and Spleen, and helps with indigestion and loose stools that are caused by a Spleen yang deficiency. Sorghum calms the body and aids insomnia. It also helps to cure coughs with white or clear discharge.

This dish nourishes the Liver and Spleen, as well as the other organs.

sorghum porridge

sorghum

Beef with Mustard Greens

½ onion, coarsely chopped

1-2 clove garlic, chopped

1 lb ground beef

1 teaspoon sea salt

½ teaspoon each black pepper, cinnamon, cumin, ground
   turmeric, ground fennel seeds

2 teaspoon butter, lard, or vegetable oil

3-4 cups mustard greens or other seasonal greens,
   coarsely chopped

1 tomato, skin peeled and diced

1 teaspoon lemon juice

1. Mix the ground beef and seasonings (salt, cumin, black pepper, cinnamon, ground turmeric, and ground fennel seeds).
2. Warm the fat or oil in a skillet over medium heat for a minute, then add the onion. Sauté the onion until softened, about 2-3 minutes. Add the chopped garlic and sauté until fragrant, about one minute.
3. Add ground beef and cook about a few minutes, stirring frequently so the ground beef doesn't clump together. The beef is done when there is only a small amount of pink meat left.
4. Add the mustard greens and tomatoes, and sauté until the mustard greens are wilted, about four minutes.
5. Add the lemon juice and serve immediately.

Functions:

*Mustard green*s are warm and spicy and go to the Spleen, Liver, Kidneys, and Lungs. They warm the body, expel cold and phlegm, regulate qi, and reduce swelling. They are used for many symptoms related to cold, wind, and dampness.

Cumin is bitter and cool. It clears the body's excess heat, inflammation, and infection, and enhances blood circulation to remove blood stasis, kills bugs, and clears skin spots.

Black pepper is hot and spicy. It acts on the Stomach, Large Intestine, and Liver. It expels cold and cleanses toxins and food poisons. It can be used for seafood poisoning and symptoms caused by cold in the digestive tract, such as stomach pain and discomfort, diarrhea, vomiting, and a lack of appetite.

Cinnamon is warm, sweet, and spicy, and acts on the Spleen, Stomach, Liver, and Kidneys. It warms any coldness in the body and induces qi circulation. It is for the common cold, abdominal pain, vomiting, diarrhea, the lack of appetite, lower back pain, soreness and feeling cold, painful periods due to stagnant cold in the digestive tract and the whole body. It is also for painful swelling and bleeding from injuries.

Turmeric is warm, bitter, and spicy, and acts on the Spleen, Liver, Heart, and Lungs. It resolves stagnant blood and reinvigorates qi circulation. It is for any symptoms caused by stagnant blood and qi circulation, such as pains in the chest, rib cage and abdomen, and from injuries, arthritis, PMS, labor, and delivery.

Fennel seeds are warm and spicy. They warm the Kidneys and Liver, help with qi circulation, and nourish the Stomach. They are for lower back pain caused by weak Kidneys, and for the pains in the rib cage and lower chest, and from injuries, arthritis, PMS, labor, delivery, and for lack of appetite, vomiting, and diarrhea.

Garlic is warm and spicy. It acts on the Spleen, Stomach, Lungs, and Large Intestine. It is for qi circulation, anti-virus, anti-fungus, removing poisons from meat and seafood, killing worms, removing stagnant food or qi, and reducing abscesses.

Tomatoes are cool, sour and a little sweet. They act on the Liver. They are for expelling excess body heat, body detoxification, and cooling down over-heated blood to calm an overactive Liver.

Lemons are cool, sour, and sweet, and act on the Stomach and Lungs. They create bodily fluid, quench thirst, nourish the Stomach, and calm the fetus.

This dish nourishes the organs, including the Liver and Spleen, replenishes qi and blood, and cleanses bodily waste.

beef with mustard greens, and toasted bread

Steamed Wheat Buns

3 cups all-purpose flour and 1 cup starter dough, or
4 cups all-purpose flour and 1 teaspoon active dry yeast
2 cups warm water

1. (**If using yeast, start here**) Mix yeast and 1/4 cup warm water, set aside for 5 minutes to let yeast activate.
2. (**If using a starter dough, start here**) Mix in 1½ cups warm water and flour. Knead until dough surface is smooth, soft, and elastic. Cover the bowl and let the dough rest in a warm place until it doubles in size, about 2 1/2 to 3 hours.
3. Slightly dust a board. Knead the dough to let the air out and until the surface of the dough is smooth. then roll the dough into a log, about 1 inch in diameter.
4. Cut the log into about one-inch-wide pieces and let the dough rise for 5 minutes.
5. Add cold water to your wok or pot. Place the buns on the steamer racks with 1 to 2 inches space between the buns. Cover.
6. Heat the pot with medium or medium low heat until the water is boiling and steam escapes from the lid. Turn to medium-high heat and steam the buns over boiling water for 15 minutes. Wait for about 5 minutes before opening the lid and serving. Serve warm.

Functions:

Wheat is close to neutral and acts on the Heart. When raised and cooked well, steamed wheat buns are very soft and easy on the digestive system.

steamed wheat buns

The raised dough for both wheat buns
and noodles

Carrot and Pumpkin Paste

1 lb pumpkin, unseeded and unskinned
1-2 carrot
½ cup walnuts, ground
2 teaspoons grated cheese, optional
2-3 teaspoons fat or cooking oil

1. Cut pumpkin and carrots into thin slices.
2. Fry the pumpkin and carrots in a pan with fat or cooking oil on medium-high heat for about two minutes.
3. Add ground walnuts and enough water (about 1½ cups) to cover the vegetables. After boiling, simmer until vegetables are soft, about 8 minutes.
4. (Optional) Add the cheese and stir until the cheese melts. Remove pan from cooktop.
5. Keep stirring until the paste is well mixed, smooth, and mushy.
6. Serve in a bowl.

Functions:

Pumpkin is warm or neutral, and sweet. It acts on the Lungs, Spleen, and Heart. It kills worms, reduces inflammation and eczema, relieves pain caused by swelling, burns, and bee stings.

Walnuts are sweet and warm. They tonify the Kidneys, provide essence, strengthen the back, warm the Lungs, and lubricate the intestines. They are for a Kidney yang deficiency, impotency, sexual dysfunctions, infertility, frequent urination, back pain, leg weakness, kidney and urinary tract stones, cough and shortness of breath, and constipation.

Carrots are sweet. Raw carrots are cool while cooked ones are neutral. Carrots act on the Spleen, Lungs, and Liver. They clear heat, detoxify the body, strengthen the Spleen, Liver, the eyes, and a weak body, and relieve cough and measles.

This dish is called eye brightening paste in Chinese because it nourishes the eyes and Liver and helps with eyesight.

carrot and pumpkin paste

Sayings on the Importance of eating and drinking:

Born to the earth are three kinds of creatures. Some are winged and fly. Some are furred and run. Still, others stretch their mouths and talk. All must eat and drink to survive.

Lu Yu, ancient Chinese philosopher, 733—804

To the ruler, the people are heaven; to the people, food is heaven.

ancient Chinese saying

Diet cures more than medicine.

ancient Chinese saying

DAY 4

Breakfast:

ham, scallion, and cheddar omelet

oatmeal with honey

milk

Morning Snack:

roasted pumpkin and/or sunflower seeds

Lunch:

shredded steak sandwich

Dinner:

adzuki bean, rice, and millet porridge

Ham, Scallion, and Cheddar Omelet

2-3 eggs
1/3 cup ham, cooked and chopped
1 tablespoon chopped green or white scallions
1 teaspoon water
salt and pepper to taste
1 tablespoon butter
1/4 cup shredded Cheddar cheese

1. In a mixing bowl, combine eggs, ham, scallions, water, salt and pepper. Gently whisk until well mixed.
2. Heat a frying pan over medium-high heat. Melt the butter and coat the pan with the melted butter.
3. Pour eggs into the pan and cook for a few seconds, until the bottom of the egg omelet is lightly set. Lift the edges of the eggs so that the uncooked portion of egg can flow under the cooked portion.
4. When eggs are set but the top is still moist, sprinkle ¾ of the cheese on top.
5. Fold one edge of the omelet over the cheese, then sprinkle the remaining cheese over the top and cook until the cheese has melted.

Functions:

Eggs are neutral and act on the Spleen, Heart, Lungs, and Kidneys. Eggs provide essence and blood and help to calm the body and mind.

Butter is warm and sweet. It provides qi and is used for a variety of ulcer and skin infections.

Cheese is neutral or warm. It acts on the Spleen, Lungs, and Liver, and provides blood, fluid, essence, and qi.

This dish nourishes all Five Organs and provides all five basic body substances.

Ham, scallion, and cheddar omelet

Oatmeal

2 cup oats (not quick cooking)
4½ cups water, or 2 ¾ cups water and 2 cup milk

1. Place oats, milk, and water in a pot. Bring to a boil and then simmer for 5-7 minutes, stirring occasionally so no oats stick to the bottom.
2. Add salt and cinnamon for taste and stir well.
3. Spoon porridge into bowls and drizzle with honey on top or mix with brown sugar.

oatmeal

Functions:

Oats are sweet and neutral (a little warm) and act on the Spleen and Heart. They strengthen the Spleen and have constraining or restricting functions, such as constraining bleeding, diarrhea, and spontaneous sweating.

Honey is neutral and acts on the Spleen and Lungs.

Brown sugar is warm and acts on the Liver, Spleen, and Stomach. It nourishes the Spleen and Liver, warms the body, and dissolves stagnate blood.

Oatmeal with honey mainly nourishes the Heart and Lungs, and oatmeal with brown sugar nourishes the Heart and Liver.

Roasted Pumpkin and/or Sunflower Seeds

1/2 - 1 cup pumpkin or sunflower seeds

1. Preheat oven broiler to 350°F.
2. Spread the seeds on a cookie sheet, in a single layer
3. Put the cookie sheet under the broiler, but not too close to the heat, for about 10 minutes, or until the seeds are brown and very crisp. Remove the shells before serving.

roasted sunflower and pumpkin seeds and brown rice

Functions:

Pumpkin seeds are sweet and warm (or neutral) and act on the Large Intestine. They kill germs and worms, control bodily fluid, help relieve swelling and produce breast milk.

Sunflower seeds are neutral and sweet. They promote circulation and expel excess heat, dampness, and wind.

Shredded Steak Sandwich

1 lb. top round steak, trimmed and cut into 1-inch chunks
1 tablespoon butter, optional
1 medium onion, finely chopped
3 cloves garlic, minced
1 tomato, skin peeled and diced
1 tablespoon brown sugar
1 tablespoon vinegar
1 teaspoon salt
1 cup beef or chicken broth, or water
4 wheat rolls, or similar types of bread

1. (Optional) Heat butter in a large nonstick skillet over medium heat until hot. Brown beef chunks on all sides.
2. Place onion and garlic in a slow cooker; place beef chunks on top. Add the diced tomato, brown sugar, vinegar, salt, and broth or water to the slow cooker. Cover and cook on high for half an hour and then on low until fork-tender, about 6 to 8 hours.
3. Remove from slow cooker. Shred the roasted beef with chopsticks or 2 forks.
4. Serve on rolls.

Functions:

Tomato is cool, sour, and a little sweet. It acts on the Liver. It is for expelling excess body heat, body detoxification, and cooling down over-heated blood to calm an overactive Liver and Heart.

Brown sugar is warm and sweet. It acts on the Liver, Spleen, and Stomach. It nourishes the Spleen and Liver, warms the body, and dissolves blood stagnation.

Vinegar is warm, sour, and sweet. It acts on the Liver and Stomach. It is used for removing stagnation, controlling bleeding, expelling waste, and killing germs.

Beef is neutral (or a little warm) and sweet. It provides qi and blood, strengthens the Spleen and Stomach, dispels dampness, and strengthens bones and tendons.

White onions act on the Lungs and Stomach.

Wheat nourishes the Heart.

The dish invigorates qi, replenishes blood, helps with circulation and expelling bodily waste.

shredded steak sandwich

Adzuki bean, Rice, and Millet Porridge

3/4 cup uncooked white rice
1/4 cup millet
1/2 cup adzuki or red beans
7 cups water
1 tablespoon sugar

1. Soak beans overnight until the beans expand and start to bubble. Or, refrigerate the beans for two hours immediately before cooking.
2. Place the water and beans in a pot. Bring to a boil, then simmer until the skins of the beans start to open. Add rice and millet and keep simmering at least half an hour until beans, rice, and millet are cooked and soft. Stir about every 15 minutes to avoid sticking to the bottom of the pot.
3. Add brown or white sugar to taste.

Adzuki bean, rice, and millet porridge

Functions:

Millet is cool, sweet, and salty. It acts on the Kidneys, Spleen, and Stomach. It is used for an overactive Stomach, vomiting, diarrhea, and difficulty in urination.

Adzuki beans are neutral, sweet, and sour. They act on the Spleen, Small Intestine, and Heart. They are for expelling excess fluid, reducing swelling, and nourishing blood.

Rice is neutral and sweet. It strengthens the Spleen, Stomach, and Lungs.

This dish is used mainly to nourish the Heart and Lungs and to expel liquid waste.

millet, adzuki beans, and rice

Sayings on Eating Habits:

> *Eat up to 70% full.*

Chinese saying

> *Eating more is not as good as chewing well.*

Chinese saying

DAY 5

Breakfast:

 bacon and egg sandwich

 oatmeal with brown sugar *(See Day 4, Page 53)*

 brown rice tea

Morning Snack:

 roasted chestnuts or sweet potato

Lunch:

 lamb stew with vegetables

 rice or steamed wheat bun

Dinner:

 rice soup with eggs and vegetables

Bacon and Egg Sandwich

For each sandwich/each serving:

>   *2 eggs, beaten*
>   *2 slices American bacon*
>   *2 slices bread, toasted, buttered*

1. Place bacon in a pan or skillet. Cook over medium-high heat until an even light brown. Drain and set aside. Reserve 1 tablespoon of bacon grease in pan for frying the eggs.
2. Pour in the eggs, cook 30 seconds. Lift the edge of eggs with a spatula to allow uncooked portion to flow underneath, 2-3 minutes or until the eggs are set. Fold the eggs to fit on the bread or on a bagel.
3. Place one piece of toasted bread on a plate. Place the fried eggs on top of the bread, top the eggs with bacon. Cover with the remaining piece of toast.

Functions:

Eggs are neutral and act on the Spleen, Heart, Lungs, and Kidneys. Eggs provide essence and blood and help to calm the body and mind.

Butter is warm and sweet. It provides qi and is useful for a variety of ulcer and skin infections.

American bacon is made from pork belly, which is neutral, acts on the Spleen, Kidneys, Lungs, Large Intestine, and Stomach, and provides blood, fluid, essence, and qi.

This dish nourishes the Spleen, Kidneys, Heart, and Lungs.

bacon and egg sandwich

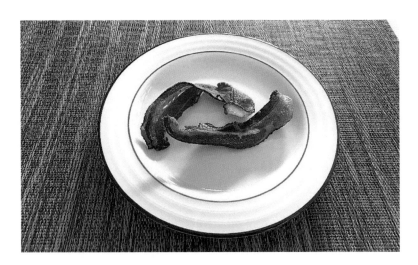

American bacon

Brown Rice Tea

brown rice

1. Preheat oven broiler to 350°F.
2. Spread the brown rice on a cookie sheet, in a single layer
3. Put the cookie sheet under the broiler, but not too close to the heat, for about 10 minutes, or until the rice is brown and very crisp.
4. To make tea, steep about 2 teaspoons of the roasted rice for a few minutes in a cup of boiling water. Store the roasted rice in a container for up to one week.

Functions:

Rice tea dries up a damp Spleen and helps digest and absorb food.

roasted brown rice

Roasted Chestnuts

chestnuts
butter, or another kind of fat or oil (optional)

1. Preheat oven to 400°F (205°C).
2. Use a sharp knife to cut a line or an "X" shape into the flat side of each chestnut.
3. (Optional) Brush the chestnuts with butter.
4. Place the chestnuts on a baking sheet and roast until the shells curl away from the nuts, about 20 minutes.
5. To serve: peel the chestnuts and discard the outer shell and the skins.

Optional: brush chestnuts with sugar water right after roasting.

roasted chestnuts

Functions:

Chestnuts are neutral, sweet, and a little salty. They act on the Spleen and Kidneys and strengthen qi. Chestnuts improve blood circulation and aid in controlling bleeding. Roasted chestnuts are used for symptoms related to Spleen and Kidney weaknesses, such as nausea and vomiting, weaknesses in the legs and knees, and abnormal bleeding.

chestnut with the spine shell

Roasted Sweet Potato

sweet potatoes

1. Preheat oven to 375° F.
2. Place sweet potatoes on a baking sheet and bake for about
   1 hour, or until tender.

Functions:

Sweet potatoes are neutral and sweet, strengthen qi, and
nourish the Spleen and Kidneys. They help with tiredness,
fatigue, feeling weak, and lacking energy.

roasted sweet potatoes

Lamb Stew with Vegetables

1 lb lamb shoulder
1-2 tablespoons butter
½ onion, diced
2 carrots
1 potato
salt and pepper to taste

1. Cut lamb shoulder, carrots, and potato into 1½-inch pieces.
2. Blanch the lamb in boiling water for a few minutes, remove, rinse, and drain.
3. In a large Dutch oven or heavy pot, heat one tablespoon of butter over medium-high heat until hot and shimmering. Brown the lamb about 5 minutes. Transfer the browned meat to a large bowl and set aside.
4. Use the leftover fat if there is enough or add up to 1 teaspoon butter. Sauté the onions for 30 seconds.
5. Add the lamb, salt, pepper, and enough water to cover. Bring to a boil and skim off any foam.
6. Reduce heat, cover, and simmer until meat is tender, about 1 hour.
7. Add the carrots and potato, then cover and continue simmering until the vegetables are cooked and the meat is very tender, about 30 minutes.

lamb stew with vegetables

Functions:

Lamb is warm and sweet and acts on the Spleen, Stomach, and Kidneys. It warms the Kidneys and the body, tonifies weakness, dispels cold, strengthens chi, nourishes blood, and increases appetite. Lamb is used for symptoms caused by a Kidney yang deficiency, such as back pain, impotence, too frequent urination, postpartum blood loss, and a lack of nursing milk.

Onions are warm, sweet, and spicy. They nourish the Stomach, help with qi circulation, kills germs, and reduce high blood lipids.

Carrots are sweet. Cooked carrots are neutral. Carrots act on the Spleen, Lungs, and Liver.

This dish strengthens a weak body, replenishes qi, nourishes blood, assist digestion. It is good for a cold day and for the symptoms of a cold body, such as coughing with white or clear discharge, cold feet and hands. More cooling vegetables, such as celery and other leafy greens, may be added as needed for balancing hot and cold.

Rice Soup with Eggs

1/2 cup uncooked white rice
5 cups water or 2 cups water and 3 cups chicken broth
1 or 2 eggs, beaten
½ cup chopped scallions
salt to taste

1. Place water (or water and chicken broth) and rice in a pot. Bring to a boil while stirring.
2. Simmer at low heat until the rice is well cooked, about 40 minutes.
3. Drip the beaten eggs slowly in to the soup, stirring constantly.
4. Add the chopped scallions and salt to taste.

Functions:

This rice soup is very easy on the digestive system and nourishes the Kidneys. It is especially good for a very sick and weak patient recovering medical treatment. Seeds and vegetables, such as ground walnuts, Chinese yam, and diced baby bok choy, may be added.

rice soup with eggs

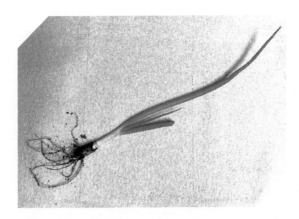

scallion with root

Sayings on daily meals:

> *Eat a nourishing breakfast, a full lunch, and little dinner.*

Chinese saying

> *Eat your breakfast alone, share your lunch with your friend, give your dinner to your enemy.*

Russian saying

DAY 6

Breakfast:

      five-color porridge

      bacon sandwich

      fermented vegetables

Morning Snack:

      mixed nuts

Lunch:

      burger

Dinner:

      black rice paste

Five-Color Porridge

1/8 cup of each: soybeans, red beans, black beans, mung beans, white (kidney) beans, and rice
6 cups water
sugar to taste

1. Soak the beans overnight and the rice for 4 hours. (Or, refrigerate the beans for 2 hours right before cooking and use 2 extra cups of water for cooking)
2. Boil the water in a pot and then add all the beans and simmer for about 40 minutes.
3. Add rice and simmer for another 40 minutes or until rice and beans are well cooked and mushy.
4. Add sugar for taste.

Five-color porridge

Functions:

Black beans are neutral and sweet and act on the Spleen, Kidneys, and Heart. They nourish the Kidneys and the Spleen, strengthen and nourish blood, regulate bodily fluid, expel wind, detoxify the body, and aid in the Kidney deficiencies with symptoms of lower back pain, knee pain, infertility, seminal emissions, ear problems, and difficulty in urination.

Mung beans are cold and sweet and act on the Heart, Liver, and Stomach. They clear heat, detoxify poison, quench thirst, promote urination, reduce swelling, aid edema in the lower limbs. They are for edema, conjunctivitis, diabetes, dysentery, fever and overheat, heatstroke, dehydration, poisons from food or medication.

White kidney beans are neutral and go to the Lungs.

This dish utilizes five different color beans to nourish all Five Organs.

Bacon Sandwich

For each sandwich/each serving:

2 slices white bread
2 slices bacon
hot sauce and honey, optional

1. Toast 2 slices of bread until dark brown.
2. Fry the bacon as crisp as you like.
3. Spread butter onto one toasted bread slice and add bacon.
4. Drizzle hot sauce and honey, as desired.
5. Place the other slice of bread on top.

Functions:

A breakfast dish with lard or butter for the energy to start the day.

bacon sandwich

Fermented Vegetables

*Use cabbage, carrot, radish, cauliflower, broccoli stems,
Napa cabbage, or other vegetables.*

1. Tear or cut the vegetables into small pieces that are no
more than 1-inch long.
2. Mix them with chopped garlic, ginger, onion, and/or a
little hot pepper.
3. Pack them as tightly as possible into a glass bottle or a clay
pot.
4. Cover vegetables in saltwater (about 2 tablespoons of salt
per 4 cups of water). Use a loose-fitting lid to cover.

Fermented vegetables are ready to eat in about two weeks.

Functions:

The vegetables are easy on the digestive system and aid in
the digestion of other foods.

fermented red cabbage and napa cabbage

Burger

1 lb. (453g) 85% lean ground beef
1 egg
1 garlic clove, chopped
½ small red or white onion, chopped
Salt and pepper (to taste)
6 burger buns
Suggested seasonings:
1 tablespoon Worcestershire sauce
1 tablespoon mustard
fresh herbs, chopped
Suggested toppings:
2 tomatoes, thinly sliced
6 slices of cheese
3-6 Lettuce leaves
1-2 pickles, sliced
Ketchup
mayonnaise
mushrooms

1. Place the ground beef in a bowl.
2. Mix the chopped onion and garlic with the ground beef.
3. Add egg, salt, pepper, and any other ingredients to the bowl (the Worcestershire sauce, mustard, and/or the chopped herbs). Mix well.
4. Using your hands, make 6 equal-sized balls.
5. Press the balls down to make flat (disk-shaped) burger patties about ½ inch thick. Make a small indent in the center of the burger with a thumb to prevent the center from swelling, leading to uneven cooking.

6. Brush the patties with a little melted butter or cooking oil before cooking.

7. Choose your cooking method. Burgers can be cooked with a broiler or grill, fried in a skillet or frying pan, barbecued, or baked. The method used depends on what you have available, what the taste and texture you prefer, and of course, your body and your living conditions.

   a. *Broiler*: Preheat the broiler (upper level) to medium heat. Broil about 6 to 7 minutes on each side, until thoroughly cooked.

   b. *Frying pan or skillet*: Use medium-low heat to fry each side of the burgers, until cooked thoroughly, about 5 minutes each side.

   c. *Barbecue grill*: Place the burgers on the grill and grill for 6 to 7 minutes on each side until thoroughly cooked.

   d. *Bake*: Place in a 350°F/180°C oven for about 20 minutes. Flip after 10 minutes. Check doneness regularly. Cook until desired tenderness or internal temperature is 150°F.

8. While the burgers are cooking, prepare the toppings:

   a. Sautee the mushrooms.

   b. Halve and toast the burger buns.

   c. Wash the lettuce and tomatoes.

   d. Thinly slice tomatoes.

9. Put one cooked burger on each piece of bread, and layer with vegetables, cheese, ketchup, and mayonnaise as desired. Place another piece of bread on top. Serve.

hamburger

Functions:

Mustard is hot and spicy and goes to the Stomach and Lungs. It warms the body, expels cold and phlegm, improves circulation, and reduces swelling. It is used for many symptoms related to cold, wind, and dampness, especially in the Stomach, and Lungs, such as vomiting, cough with white discharge, arthritis, and amenorrhea.

Burgers replenish qi, nourish blood, and expel weather pathogens (cold, heat, damp, dry, and wind).

Black Rice Paste

1 cup uncooked black rice
5 cups water

1. Soak the black rice in 1½ cup water overnight.
2. Grind the rice with the water using a food processor.
3. Place the rest of the water and the ground rice in a pot. Bring to a boil.
4. Turn down the heat to simmer. Stir the bottom of the pot to prevent the rice from burning.
5. Simmer for 30 minutes or longer, until the black rice becomes mushy and mixed with the water.

black rice paste

Functions:

Black rice is neutral and sweet and acts on the Spleen, Stomach, Kidneys, Lungs, and Liver. It is called "blood rice" because it nourishes blood and is for blood and yin deficiencies, especially for women who have just given birth. Black rice is also called "long life rice" because it nourishes all major organs (Spleen, Kidneys, Lungs, and Liver) that create, manage, or store life energy.

black rice

Sayings on the Human Ignorance:

> *Real knowledge is to know
> the extent of one's ignorance.*

Confucius, ancient Chinese philosopher, 551-479 B.C.

> *People do not die from
> disease but from ignorance.*

Hiroshi Nakajima, director-general of the World Health
Organization, 1928-2013

DAY 7

Breakfast:

>shaved steak omelet

>muffin

>milk

Morning Snack:

>mixed nuts

Lunch:

>steamed meatballs

Dinner:

>rice soup with eggs and chicken broth (*See Day 5, Page 71*)

Shaved Steak Omelet

½ lb shaved or slivered steak (boneless rib-eye)
3 eggs
1 tablespoon butter or olive oil
1 bell pepper, chopped
1/2 sweet onion, chopped
5 small mushrooms, chopped
1/4 cup provolone cheese, grated, sliced thin, or shredded
salt and pepper to taste

1. Melt the butter in a frying pan over medium heat. Add the onion, pepper, and mushrooms, stirring frequently, until soft and golden brown, about 15 minutes. Transfer to a bowl.
2. Add 1/2 tablespoon of butter to a pan over medium-high heat. Add the steak slices, separating layers so they do not clump together, and brown on all sides.
3. Add vegetables. Season with salt and pepper. Add provolone. Once the cheese melts into the mixture, remove the mixture, and transfer back to the bowl.
4. Add the butter to the pan over medium heat. Crack the eggs into a bowl and beat with chopsticks or a fork. Season with salt and pepper. Add the eggs. Once the underside has lightly browned, flip with a spatula. Add the filling. Fold one side over to cover filling, and gently slide omelet onto plate.

shaved steak omelet

Functions:

This steak omelet is loaded with protein and energy and acts on all Five Organs.

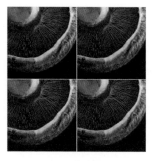

mushrooms

Muffin

1/3 cup sugar
½ teaspoon salt
1 teaspoon grated orange peel
1 cup of starter dough
1 ½ cups flour
1/2 cup warm milk or kefir
1/4 cup warm water
1 egg
1/3 cup butter, melted

For glaze (optional):
1 teaspoon grated orange peel
½ cup white sugar
1 tablespoon orange juice

1. In a bowl, mix salt, orange peel, sugar, and 1 cup of the flour.
2. Combine milk, water, starter dough, egg, and butter.
3. Gradually add the liquid to the flour mixture, mixing thoroughly.
4. Stir in the rest of the flour to make a stiff batter. Cover and let rise in a warm place until doubled in size, about 2 to 3 hours.
5. Gently knead the dough. Spoon into greased muffin pans. Bake at 375 degrees about 20 minutes. Remove from pans and cool on wire rack.
6. (Optional) Drizzle with an orange glaze made by combining the white sugar, grated orange peel, and orange juice.

muffins

Functions:

Orange peels are warm, bitter, and spicy. They go to the
Spleen, Stomach, and Lungs, and help with qi circulation.
They harmonize the Middle Warmer (the Spleen and
Stomach), dry dampness, and dissolve phlegm. They are for
qi stagnation in the Middle Warmer with symptoms such as
nausea and vomiting, fullness, distention, bloating,
stomachache, belching, and poor appetite. They help with the
accumulation of phlegm and dampness in the Middle Warmer
with symptoms such as fatigue, low appetite, loose stool,
diarrhea, abdominal fullness, chest oppression, and a greasy,
thick tongue coating. They are also for the accumulation of
phlegm and qi in the Lungs with symptoms such as cough

with profuse phlegm, wheezing, dyspnea, and stifling sensation in the chest.

Goes nicely with the steak omelet. This muffin helps in digesting meat and strengthening the body.

Steamed Meatballs

1 lb ground beef or pork
2 tablespoons soy sauce
1 teaspoon five-spice seasoning
1 cup chopped white or green scallions,
A few pieces of thinly sliced ginger, chopped
1 cup milk or water
1 teaspoon salt
1 cup breadcrumbs or flour
cooking oil for frying

1. Thoroughly mix ground meat, water or milk, soy sauce, five-spice seasoning, scallions, ginger, and salt. Then add the breadcrumbs (or flour) and mix well again.
2. Separate the mixture into four parts, shape each part into a large ball.
3. Heat enough cooking oil in a frying pot to cover at least one meatball. Fry the meatballs until their surfaces are brown. Place the fried meatballs on a deep plate. Top the meatballs with thinly sliced ginger and scallions, as desired.
4. Use a steamer to steam the meatballs on a plate at high heat for 15 minutes.
5. Serve the meatballs and the soup warm.

Functions:

Steamed meatballs are very soft. They are more balanced (neutral) in energy and easier to digest than many other meat dishes.

steamed meatballs

Sayings about Healing, Energy, and Life Energy:

> *The hardest part of healing is not healing itself but the imbedded beliefs on health in the modern world.*

Julia Sun, self-healing expert

> *Health is life energy in abundance. With the right energy in the right place, every disease can be preventable and curable.*

Julia Sun, self-healing expert

> *If you want to understand everything, think in turns of energy and its movement.*

Julia Sun, self-healing expert

Food Index

List of foods mentioned in this recipe book with their energy properties. For other foods and their energy properties, check out my book *Total Life Energy Plan – How to Cultivate Life Energy for Health and Vitality,* and Traditional Chinese Medicine dictionaries on herbs. The book *Total Life Energy Plan* (ISBN number 978-0999623237) is available on Amazon, public libraries, https://totallifeenergyplan.com/, and many other websites.

Printed in Great Britain
by Amazon

42506410R00055